LoVe

LoVe

Poems chosen by
Fiona Waters

MACMILLAN

For Bryan
'. . . let the winds of the heavens dance between you.'
Kahil Gibran

First published 2002
by PanMacmillan Limited
20 New Wharf Road, London N1 9RR
Basingstoke and Oxford
www.panmacmillan.com

Associated companies throughout the world

ISBN 0 333 90348 X

3 5 7 9 8 6 4 2

A CIP catalogue record for this book is available from the British Library.

Printed in China

Contents

The Power of Love

It can alter things:
The stormy scowl can become
Suddenly a smile.

The knuckly bunched fist
May open like a flower,
Tender a caress.

Beneath its bright warmth
Black ice of suspicion melts;
Danger is dazzled.

A plain and dull face
Astounds with its radiance
And sudden beauty.

Ordinary things –
Teacups, spoons and sugar-lumps –
Become magical.

The locked door opens;
Inside are leaves and moonlight;
You are welcomed in.

Its delicate strength
Can lift the heaviest heart
And snap hostile steel.

It gives eloquence
To the dumb tongue, makes plain speech
Blaze like poetry.

Vernon Scannell

If Love Was Jazz

If love was jazz,
I'd be dazzled
By its razzmatazz.

If love was a sax,
I'd melt in its brassy flame
Like wax.

If love was a guitar,
I'd pluck its six strings,
Eight to the bar.

If love was a trombone,
I'd feel its slow
Slide, right down my backbone.

If love was a drum,
I'd be caught in its snare,
Kept under its thumb.

If love was a trumpet,
I'd blow it.

If love was jazz,
I'd sing its praises,
Like Larkin has.

But love isn't jazz.
It's an organ recital.
Eminently worthy,
Not nearly as vital.

If love was jazz,
I'd always want more.
I'd be a regular
On that smoky dance-floor.

Linda France

The First Day

I wish I could remember the first day,
First hour, first moment of your meeting me;
If bright or dim the season, it might be
Summer or winter for aught I can say.
So unrecorded did it slip away,
So blind was I to see and to foresee,
So dull to mark the budding of my tree
That would not blossom yet for many a May.

If only I could recollect it! Such
A day or days! I let it come and go
As traceless as a thaw of bygone snow.
It seemed to mean so little, meant so much!
If only now I could recall that touch,
First touch of hand in hand! Did one but know!

Christina Rossetti

Sea Song

Come sail the whispering seas, my love,
Come drift on the tides with me;
For I still long for the wild waves' song
And the silver fish of the sea.

Oh I'd sail the sighing seas, my love,
Where the wild weeds gently glide;
But I'm afraid of the forest shade
Where the silent fishes hide.

Don't fear the sauntering seas, my love,
As they dance beneath the breeze;
In the moonlit foam we'll make our home
Like the silver fish of the seas.

Oh I'll sail the rolling seas, my love,
And sigh for the cry of the wind;
But what if I weep on the ocean deep
To tread a greener land?

Oh you'll love the roaring seas, my love!
Come ride the swell with me,
Where the breaking sky is drawn to die
With the silver fish of the sea.

If I ride the raging seas, my love,
Then will you follow me?
Or will you stay till your dying day
With the silver fish of the sea?

Oh I must ride the wild, wild seas
And you must let me be;
Till my dying day I'll roam the spray
With the silver fish of the sea.

Judith Nicholls

Blackberry Sweet

Black girl black girl
lips as curved as cherries
full as grape bunches
sweet as blackberries

Black girl black girl
when you walk you are
magic as a rising bird
or a falling star

Black girl black girl
what's your spell to make
the heart in my breast
jump stop shake

Dudley Randall

The Duke of Fire and the Duchess of Ice

Passionate love for the Duke of Fire
the Duchess of Ice felt.
One kiss was her heart's desire,
but with one kiss she would melt.

She dreamed of him in his red pantaloons,
in his orange satin blouse,
in his crimson cravat,
in his tangerine hat,
in his vermilion dancing shoes.

One kiss, one kiss,
lips of flame on frost,
one kiss, pure bliss,
and never count the cost.

She woke. She went to the bathroom.
She took a freezing shower —
her body as pale as a stalagmite,
winter's frailest flower.

Then the Duke of Fire stood there,
radiant, ablaze with love,
and the Duchess of Ice cared nothing
for anything in the world.

She spoke his name,
her voice was snow,
kissed him, kissed him again,
and in his warm, passionate arms
turned to water, tears, rain.

Carol Ann Duffy

Like a Flame

Raising up
from my weeding
of ripening cane

my eyes
make four
with this man

there ain't
no reason
to laugh

but
I laughing
in confusion

his hands
soft his words
quick his lips
curling as in
prayer

I nod

I like this man

Tonight
I go to meet him
like a flame

Grace Nichols

A Birthday

My heart is like a singing bird
    Whose nest is in a watered shoot;
My heart is like an apple-tree
    Whose boughs are bent with thickset fruit;
My heart is like a rainbow shell
    That paddles in a halcyon sea;
My heart is gladder than all these
    Because my love is come to me.

Raise me a dais of silk and down;
    Hang it with vair and purple dyes;
Carve it in doves and pomegranates,
    And peacocks with a hundred eyes;
Work it in gold and silver grapes,
    In leaves and silver fleurs-de-lys;
Because the birthday of my life
    Is come, my love is come to me.

Christina Rossetti

The minute I heard my first love story

The minute I heard my first love story
I started looking for you not knowing
how blind that was.

Lovers don't finally meet somewhere.
They're in each other all along.

Rumi, translated by Coleman Barks
with John Moyne

The Confirmation

Yes, yours, my love, is the right human face.
I in my mind had waited for this long,
Seeing the false and searching for the true,
Then found you as a traveller finds a place
Of welcome suddenly amid the wrong
Valleys and rocks and twisting roads. But you,
What shall I call you? A fountain in a waste,
A well of water in a country dry,
Or anything that's honest and good, an eye
That makes the whole world bright. Your open heart,
Simple with giving, gives the primal deed,
The first good world, the blossom, the blowing seed,
The hearth, the steadfast land, the wandering sea.
Not beautiful or rare in every part,
But like yourself, as they were meant to be.

Edwin Muir

Words, for E

The sky is blue, or something. Anyway, it's there.
Your words are hands, stroking me, stroking the sky,
Blue sky, names, people. It's marvellous, I'm king,
And your words are a line of ships. The guns fire.
Blue sky, names, people. I take the salute.

You are beautiful, sometimes. Now.
I feel for words for you. The ship rising, falling,
The horizon, a line rising, falling, behind your hair.
Words rise, spray. I like to think of you as giving
Structure. A gentleness. A constancy.

Tom Leonard

Love Song

If I could write words
Like leaves on an autumn forest floor
What a bonfire my letters would make.
If I could speak words of water
You would drown when I said
'I love you'.

Spike Milligan

The Silver Hat

Loving you
is like wearing
a silver hat.
Everywhere I go
people stop me
and ask, 'What's that
remarkable thing
on your head?'

I used to see
other people
wearing silver hats
but never thought
I'd be lucky enough
to get one.
I thought I was
destined to be
one of those unhappy,
unhatted
people.
But now . . .

Now I visit friends
just to show them
how wonderful I look.
Last night,
for example,
I went to see
a silver-hatted person
I hadn't seen for ages.
We spoke about many
hat-related topics.

On the way home
I passed your house
and, suddenly,
found myself
writing a note
and slipping it
under your door.

In the morning
you'll find a
piece of paper
on your doormat.
I wonder what
you'll think when
you read,
'Please
don't ever
take your
hat away.'

Philip Ridley

LoVe

The Lover Writes a One-Word Poem

You!

Gavin Ewart

The Negro Girl

Black delicate face
among a forest
of white pasty faces.

Her eyelids closed
for a moment only
as she stood by the door
of the subway car,

and in that instant
my lips had hurdled
the crowd and planted
the warmest of kisses
on those folded dark petals,

then vanished as quickly
before the quick eyes
could open to discover
her unknown impetuous
delirious lover.

Raymond Souster

The Corner of the Field

Here the young lover, on his elbow raised,
Looked at his happy girl with grass surrounded,
And flicked the spotted beetle from her wrist:
She, with her head thrown back, at the heaven gazed,
At Suffolk clouds, serene and slow and mounded;
Then calmly smiled at him before they kissed.

Frances Cornford

The Kiss

'I saw you take his kiss!' ''Tis true.'
　　　'O, modesty!' ''Twas strictly kept:
He thought me asleep; at least I knew
　　　He thought I thought he thought I slept.'

Coventry Patmore

Party

Sitting on the stairs,
you tell me that when you were five
a boy called David Bird tried to kiss you,
missed, and fell into a bed of nettles.

I want to kiss you now,
but what would I fall off,
and what would I fall into?

Too late I move, indecisively,
and fall into the nettles.

Someone takes you gently by the hand,
smoothes your hair,
leads you back into the party.

Adrian Henri

If Thou Must Love Me, Let It Be for Nought

If thou must love me, let it be for nought
Except for love's sake only. Do not say
'I love her for her smile – her look – her way
Of speaking gently, – for a trick of thought
That falls in well with mine, and certes brought
A sense of pleasant ease on such a day' –
For these things in themselves, beloved, may
Be changed, or change for thee, – and love, so wrought,
May be unwrought so. Neither love me for
Thine own dear pity's wiping my cheeks dry, –
A creature might forget to weep, who bore
Thy comfort long, and lose thy love thereby!
But love me for love's sake, that evermore
Though may'st love on, through love's eternity.

Elizabeth Barrett Browning

I'm in Love with the Weather Lady

I'm in love with the Weather Lady
I could sit here and watch her all day
I don't care if earthquakes are forecast
I just want to hear what she'll say

I'm in love with the Weather Lady
Can't wait until after the news
You can never see below her knees
Perhaps she doesn't wear shoes

I'm in love with the Weather Lady
Her smile drives the black clouds away
There's a deep depression if I miss her
A cold front that lasts through the day

I'm in love with the Weather Lady
I watch her through lunchtime and tea
I'm in love with the Weather Lady
But I don't think she knows about me.

Adrian Henri

Frog

There's a prince in every frog
croaking in the misty bog.

Riad Nourallah

Prayer to St Catherine*

St Catherine, St Catherine, O lend me thine aid,
And grant that I never may die an old maid.

A husband, St Catherine,
A *good* one, St Catherine;
But arn-a-one better than
Narn-a-one, St Catherine.

Sweet St Catherine,
A husband, St Catherine,
Handsome, St Catherine,
Rich, St Catherine.

Anonymous

*St Catherine is the patron saint of spinsters

He loves my hair

serious Simon
met a poet
going to a gig

said serious Simon
to the poet
'is your hair a wig?'

said the poet
to now smiling Simon
'touch it, if you will'

since then his hand
hasn't left her hair
and they are laughing still

Jean 'Binta' Breeze

In a Bath Teashop

'Let us not speak, for the love we bear one another
     Let us hold hands and look.'
She, such a very ordinary little woman;
     He, such a thumping crook;
But both, for a moment, little lower than the angels
     In the teashop's ingle-nook.

John Betjeman

I Will Make You Brooches

I will make you brooches and toys for your delight
Of bird-song at morning and star-shine at night.
I will make a palace fit for you and me
Of green days in forests and blue days at sea.

I will make my kitchen, and you shall keep your room,
Where white flows the river and bright blows the broom,
And you shall wash your linen and keep your body white
In rainfall at morning and dewfall at night.

And this shall be for music when no one else is near,
the fine song for singing, the rare song to hear!
That only I remember, that only you admire,
Of the broad road that stretches and the roadside fire.

Robert Louis Stevenson

My Box

My box is made of golden oak,
my lover's gift to me.
He fitted hinges and a lock
of brass and a bright key.
He made it out of winter nights,
sanded and oiled and planed,
engraved inside the heavy lid
in brass, a golden tree.

In my box are twelve black books
where I have written down
how we have sanded, oiled and planed,
planted a garden, built a wall,
seen jays and goldcrests, rare red kites,
found the wild heartsease, drilled a well,
harvested apples and words and days
and planted a golden tree.

On an open shelf I keep my box.
Its key is in the lock.
I leave it there for you to read,
or them, when we are dead,
how everything is slowly made,
how slowly things made me,
a tree, a lover, words, a box,
books and a golden tree.

Gillian Clarke

Flowers

Some men never think of it.
You did. You'd come along
And say you'd nearly brought me flowers
But something had gone wrong.

The shop was closed. Or you had doubts –
The sort that minds like ours
Dream up incessantly. You thought
I might not want your flowers.

It made me smile and hug you then.
Now I can only smile.
But, look, the flowers you nearly brought
Have lasted all this while.

Wendy Cope

Now You Will Feel No Rain

Now you will feel no rain,
for each of you will be a shelter to the other.

Now you will feel no cold,
for each of you will be warmth to the other.

Now there is no loneliness for you;
now there is no more loneliness.

Now you are two bodies,
but there is only one life before you.

Go now to your dwelling place,
to enter into your days together.

And may your days be good
and long on the earth.

Apache song

The Bargain

My true love hath my heart, and I have his,
By just exchange one for another given:
I hold his dear, and mine he cannot miss,
There never was a better bargain driven:
My true love hath my heart, and I have his.

His heart in me keeps him and me in one,
My heart in him his thoughts and senses guides:
He loves my heart, for once it was his own,
I cherish his because in me it bides:
My true love hath my heart, and I have his.

Sir Philip Sidney

The Female Highwayman

Priscilla on one summer's day
Dressed herself up in men's array;
With a brace of pistols by her side
All for to meet her true love she did ride.

And when she saw her true love there
She boldly bade him for to stand.
'Stand and deliver, kind sir,' she said,
'For if you don't I'll shoot you dead.'

And when she'd robbed him of all his store,
She said, 'Kind sir, there's one thing more;
The diamond ring I've seen you wear,
Deliver that and your life I'll spare.'

'That ring,' said he, 'my true love gave;
My life I'll lose but that I'll save.'
Then, being tender-hearted like a dove,
She rode away from the man she love.

Anon they walked upon the green,
And he spied his watch pinned to her clothes,
Which made her blush, which made her blush
Like a full, blooming rose.

''Twas me who robbed you on the plain,
So here's your watch and your gold again.
I did it only for to see
If you would really faithful be.
And now I'm sure this is true,
I also give my heart to you.'

Anonymous

The Icingbus

the littleman
with the hunchbackedback
creptto his feet
to offer his seat
to the blindlady

people gettingoff
steered carefully around
the black mound
of his back
as they would a pregnantbelly

the littleman
completely unaware
of the embarrassment behind
watched as the blindlady
fingered out her fare

. . . .

40   Love

muchlove later he suggested that instead
ofa wedding-cake they shouldhave a miniaturebus
made outof icing but she laughed
andsaid that buses werefor travelling in
and notfor eating and besides
you cant taste shapes.

Roger McGough

Song of the Rain

Night
And the yellow pleasure of candle-light . . .
Old brown books and the kind fine face of the clock
Fogged in the veils of the fire – its cuddling tock.
The cat,
Greening her eyes on the flame-litten mat;
Wickedly wakeful she yawns at the rain
Bending the roses over the pane,
And a bird in my heart begins to sing
Over and over the same sweet thing –

Safe in the house with my boyhood's love,
And our children asleep in the attic above.

Hugh McCrae

Human Affection

Mother, I love you so.
Said the child, I love you more than I know.
She laid her head on her mother's arm,
And the love between them kept them warm.

Stevie Smith

Bearhug

Griffin calls to come and kiss him goodnight
I yell OK. Finish something I'm doing,
then something else, walk slowly round
the corner to my son's room.
He is standing arms outstretched
waiting for a bearhug. Grinning.

Why do I give my emotion an animal's name,
give it that dark squeeze of death?
This is the hug which collects
all his small bones and his warm neck against me.
The thin tough body under the pyjamas
locks to me like a magnet of blood.

How long was he standing there
like that, before I came?

Michael Ondaatje

Two Small Boys and an Elephant

That was hopeless love, when the brothers gazed
at elephants at the Zoo.

One turned great grey legs and back on them
as elephants do.

Brothers gazed after elephants with love
and then, on cue,

returned to loving ice creams
as small boys do.

Fred Sedgwick

Walking Away

It is eighteen years ago, almost to the day –
A sunny day with the leaves just turning,
The touch-lines new-ruled – since I watched you play
Your first game of football, then, like a satellite
Wrenched from its orbit, go drifting away

Behind a scatter of boys. I can see
You walking away from me towards the school
With the pathos of a half-fledged thing set free
Into a wilderness, the gait of one
Who finds no path where the path should be.

That hesitant figure, eddying away
Like a winged seed loosened from its parent stem,
Has something I never quite grasp to convey
About nature's give-and-take – the small, the scorching
Ordeals which fire one's irresolute clay.

I have had worse partings, but none that so
Gnaws at my mind still. Perhaps it is roughly
Saying what God alone could perfectly show –
How selfhood begins with a walking away,
And love is proved in the letting go.

C. Day Lewis

The Railings

You came to watch me playing cricket once.
Quite a few of the fathers did.
At ease, outside the pavilion
they could while away a Saturday afternoon.
Joke with the masters, urge on
their flannelled offspring. But not you.

Fielding deep near the boundary
I saw you through the railings.
You were embarassed when I waved
and moved out of sight down the road.
When it was my turn to bowl though
I knew you'd still be watching.

Third ball, a wicket, and three more followed.
When we came in at the end of the innings
the other dads applauded and joined us for tea.
Of course, you had gone by then. Later,
you said you'd found yourself there by accident.
Just passing. Spotted me through the railings.

***

Speech-days * Prize-givings * School-plays
The Twenty-first * The Wedding * The Christening
You would find yourself there by accident.
Just passing. Spotted me through the railings.

Roger McGough

Those Winter Sundays

Sundays too my father got up early
and put his clothes on in the blueblack cold,
then with cracked hands that ached
from labour in the weekday weather made
banked fires blaze. No one ever thanked him.

I'd wake and hear the cold splintering, breaking.
When the rooms were warm, he'd call,
and slowly I would rise and dress,
fearing the chronic angers of that house,

Speaking indifferently to him,
who had driven out the cold
and polished my good shoes as well.
What did I know, what did I know
of love's austere and lonely offices?

Robert Hayden

I Saw a Sad Man in a Field

I saw a sad man in a field
Working,
Each day I ran alongside
Waving.

My father said the man was bad
Wicked,
Forbade me ever more to wave
Friendly.

I walked to school beside the field
Crying.
My friend he understood I felt
Sadly.

He was a German, prisoner
Homesick,
He had a little girl like me
Grieving.

Afraid I walked up to the fence
Gazing,
He smiled and shook his head at me
Smiling.

He was young and blond and nice
Enemy,
I loved him very much indeed
Hurting, hurting.

Joan Batchelor

To My Daughter

Bright clasp of her whole hand around my finger,
My daughter, as we walk together now.
All my life I'll feel a ring invisibly
Circle this bone with shining: when she is grown
Far from today as her eyes are far already.

Stephen Spender

Growing Pain

The boy was barely five years old.
We sent him to the little school
And left him there to learn the names
Of flowers in jam jars on the sill
And learn to do as he was told.
He seemed quite happy there until
Three weeks afterwards, at night,
The darkness whimpered in his room.
I went upstairs, switched on his light,
And found him wide awake, distraught,
Sheets mangled and his eiderdown
Untidy carpet on the floor.
I said, 'Why can't you sleep? A pain?'
He snuffled, gave a little moan,
And then he spoke a single word:
'Jessica.' The sound was blurred.
'Jessica? What do you mean?'
'A girl at school called Jessica,
She hurts –' he touched himself between
The heart and stomach '– she has been
Aching here and I can see her.'
Nothing I had read or heard

Instructed me in what to do.
I covered him and stroked his head.
'The pain will go, in time,' I said.

Vernon Scannell

I'd Never Fall in Love with a Girl

I'd never fall in love with a *girl*.

I might fall in love with my new tracksuit top
or my bike
or my mum –
but I'd never fall in love with a *girl*.

I might fall in love with my old casie football
or Liverpool FC
or Auntie Sandra
(she's really nice,
but she's grown up,
and anyway she's married to my Uncle Eddie),
But I'd never fall in love with a *girl*.

I might fall in love with Tessa Jones,
but she's not a girl at all really.
She can run faster,
climb higher, fight harder
and kick a ball further
than any of the boys.

I might even fall in love
with my mate Stephen
(if he'd let me, that is) –
except he can't run as fast,
or climb as high, or fight as hard,
or kick a ball as far
as Tessa Jones . . .

But I'd *never* fall in love
WITH A GIRL.

Dave Ward

Taking the Plunge

One day a boy said to a girl in a swimming pool
'I'm going to dive in, are you?' She replied
'No thanks. I bet you can't anyway.' So the boy
got on the diving board and dived and said
'See.' The girl replied 'Flipping eck!'
  (Simon Wilkinson, Margaret Wix Junior School, St Albans.)

Flipping eck, cor blimey, strewth,
You're my hero, that's the honest truth.

Lummy, crikey, lordy lord,
It's a long way down from that diving board.

Itchy beard and stone the crows,
Don't you get chlorine up your nose?

Luv a duck and strike me pink,
You're slicker than the soap in the kitchen sink.

Knock me down with a sparrow's feather,
How about us going out together?

Groovy, t'riffic, brill and smashing,
Me 'n' you, we could start things splashing.
Wotcha cocky, tara, see ya,
Meet me for a Coke in the cafeteria.

Halleluja and Amen,
If you like this poem you can read it again.

John Mole

Oranges

The first time I walked
With a girl, I was twelve,
Cold, and weighted down
With two oranges in my jacket.
December. Frost cracking
Beneath my steps, my breath
Before me, then gone,
As I walked toward
Her house, the one whose
Porch light burned yellow
Night and day, in any weather.
A dog barked at me, until
She came out pulling
At her gloves, face bright
With rouge. I smiled,
Touched her shoulder, and led
Her down the street, across
A used car lot and a line
Of newly planted trees,
Until we were breathing
Before a drugstore. We
Entered, the tiny bell

Bringing a saleslady
Down a narrow aisle of goods.
I turned to the candies
Tiered like bleachers,
And asked what she wanted –
Light in her eyes, a smile
Starting at the corners
Of her mouth. I fingered
A nickel in my pocket,
And when she lifted a chocolate
That cost a dime,
I didn't say anything.
I took the nickel from
My pocket, then an orange,
And set them quietly on
The counter. When I looked up,
The lady's eyes met mine,
And held them, knowing
Very well what it was all
About.
Outside
A few cars hissing past,
Fog hanging like old
Coats between the trees.

I took my girl's hand
In mine for two blocks,
Then released it to let
Her unwrap the chocolate.
I peeled my orange
That was so bright against
The grey of December
That, from some distance,
Someone might have thought
I was making a fire in my hands.

Gary Soto

Lizzie Pitofsky Poem

I can't get enoughsky
Of Lizzie Pitofsky
I love her so much that it hurts.
I want her so terrible
I'd give her my gerbil
Plus twenty-two weeks of desserts.

I know that it's lovesky
'Cause Lizzie Pitofsky
Is turning me into a saint
I smell like a rose,
I've stopped picking my nose,
And I practically never say 'Ain't'.

I don't push and shovesky
'Cause Lizzie Pitofsky
Likes boys who are gentle and kind.
I'm not throwing rocks
And I'm changing my socks
(And to tell you the truth I don't mind)

Put tacks in my shoes,
Feed me vinegar juice,
And do other mean, bad, awful stuffsky.
But promise me this:
I won't die without kiss-
ing my glorious Lizzie Pitofsky.

Judith Viorst

First Love

Everyone says that my girlfriend Gemma
Is big for her age
And that what we apparently feel for each other
Is only a stage.

But what, when they grumble, I have to agree
Is as plain as day
Is that Gemma tends to throw her big weight about
Every which way.

Once when I showed her a shed in our garden
She climbed on the roof
And then when I wasn't expecting leapt down like
an Amazon.
Strewth!

All of my breath was completely knocked out of me,
All of my puff,
But just to have Gemma landing on top of me
Was enough.

John Mole

First Kiss

My problem is
I don't know how
to kiss.

What happens
to your teeth?

Will our lips stick?

Should you blow?

What if I spit
and dribble?

I'd like to
but hope
I don't giggle . . .

I might
Just decide
To say no though.

Joan Poulson

'Till Playtime Do us Part
and the Lovehearts Are All Eaten

One kiss and that was it.
Love.
I say one kiss but it wasn't even a proper one.
He went to kiss her on the cheek,
she turned round dead embarrassed
so all he got was a mouthful of hair . . . and a nose
bleed.
But it was still love.

One kiss behind the school wall at playtime
and that was it.
Love. True love.
They decided to get married.

They'd bring each other presents.
 He'd bring her his favourite Football Team swap cards,
his seventy fiver conker and his best set of tadpoles.
She'd give him her favourite lucky charm
(a plastic My Little Pony on a key ring),
and sweets covered in fluff from the bottom of her

schoolbag.
So he gave up playing football at playtimes
and she tied big knots in her skipping rope.

They'd sit for hours and hours and hours
gazing deeply into each other's eyes
until they went cross-eyed and dizzy,
eating packets and packets and packets of lovehearts
reading the messages out to each other in dead soppy
    voices:

'Be mine forever'
'Hiya cutie'
'Love ya lots 'n' lots'
'You snog dead good'

Nine and a half years old and they got married,
curtain rings and stolen flowers
muddy-kneed and laughing,
the whole class drank Dandelion and Burdock.
Their friends told them it wouldn't last.
They were right.
Two weeks later she left him.
She went off with a brand new bike

and fell in love with a pop star from Manchester
(designer clothes, no spots and toothpaste smile).
So he went off with the school football team
and dreamed of scoring the winning goal at Wembley.

Paul Cookson

Studup

'Owaryer?'
'Imokay.'
'Gladtwearit.'
'Howbowchew?'
'Reelygrate.'
'Binwaytinlong?'
'Longinuff.'
'Owlongubinear?'
'Boutanour.'
'Thinkeelturnup?'
'Aventaclue.'
'Dewfancyim?'
'Sortalykim.'
'Wantadrinkorsummat?'
'Thanksilestayabit.'
'Soocherself.'
'Seeyalater.'
'Byfernow.'

Barrie Wade

Smiling

Her eyes twinkled like the sun
catching the spokes
of a brand new bike wheel.
When she laughed she cupped her hands
over her mouth like you do
when you catch a butterfly.
Sometimes she touched my arm
when we talked
and I felt like I'd won Olympic Gold
just for being me.
When I fooled around she'd tell me off
but I knew she didn't mean it.
In assembly I'd sit next to her
and the sound of her breathing
made everybody disappear.
In English I loved the way
she held her hair
when she leaned over a book.
And I wished I was that book;
close and full of all the right words.
Then one night after the school disco
she asked me to walk her home

and I decided to tell her that I loved her.
It was cold out but I left my coat open
so that she could still see my new shirt.
We stopped walking by the old
garages at the bottom of her road
and she told me how she really liked me
and that she could really talk to me.
Before I could say anything she said
It's great to have a boy just as a friend.
JUST AS A FRIEND . . .
I felt like every bad thing that had happened
to me was happening again all at once.
The next thing I know
she was closing her front door
and I was doing the hardest thing
I've ever done:
I was smiling.

Stephen Clarke

Stepmother

My stepmother
   is really nice.
She ought to wear
   a label.
I don't come in
   with a latch key, now –
my tea is on
   the table.
She doesn't nag at me
   or shout.
I often hear her
   singing.
I'm glad my dad
   had wedding bells
and I hope
   they go on ringing.

Stepmothers
   in fairy tales
are hard and cold
   as iron.
There isn't a lie
   they wouldn't tell,
or a trick
   they wouldn't try on.
But MY stepmother's
   warm and true;
she's kind and cool,
   and clever –
Yes! I've a *wicked*
   stepmother –
and I hope she stays
   for ever!

Jean Kenward

My cat and i

Girls are simply the prettiest things
My cat and i believe
And we're always saddened
When it's time for them to leave

We watch them titivating
(that often takes a while)
And though they keep us waiting
My cat & i just smile.

We like to see them to the door
Say how sad it couldn't last
Then my cat and i go back inside
And talk about the past.

Roger McGough

This cat

This cat
she expects love.
Demands it
stalks it
feels she has a right to it.
She is not ashamed –
I wish I were more like this cat.

Gabriela Pearse

Wearing the collar

I live with a lady and four cats
and some days we all get
along.

some days I have trouble with
one of the
cats.

other days I have trouble with
two of the cats.

other days,
three.

some days I have trouble with
all four of the
cats

and the lady:

ten eyes looking at me
as if I was a dog.

Charles Bukowski

Message

Pick up the phone before it is too late
And dial my number. There's no time to spare –
Love is already turning into hate
And very soon I'll start to look elsewhere.

Good, old-fashioned men like you are rare –
You want to get to know me at a rate
That's guaranteed to drive me to despair.
Pick up the phone before it is too late.

Well, wouldn't it be nice to consummate
Our friendship while we've still got teeth and hair?
Just bear in mind that you are forty-eight
And dial my number. There's no time to spare.

Another kamikaze love affair?
No chance. This time I'll have to learn to wait
But one more day is more than I can bear –
Love is already turning into hate.

Of course, my friends say I exaggerate
And dramatize a lot. That may be fair
But it is no fun being in this state
And very soon I'll start to look elsewhere.

I know you like me but I wouldn't dare
Ring you again. Instead I'll concentrate
On sending thought-waves through the London air
And, if they reach you, please don't hesitate –
Pick up the phone.

Wendy Cope

The Pros and the Cons

He'll be pleased if I phone to ask him how he is.
It will make me look considerate and he likes
  considerate people.

He'll be reassured to see that I haven't lost interest,
which might make him happy and then I'll have done
  him a favour.

If I phone him right now I'll get to speak to him sooner
than I will if I sit around waiting for him to phone me.

He might not want to phone me from work in case
  someone hears him
and begins (or continues) to suspect that there's
  something between us.

If I want to and don't, aren't I being a bit immature?
We're both adults. Does it matter, with adults, who
  makes the first move?

But there's always the chance he'll back off if I come on
    too strong
The less keen I appear, the more keen he's likely to be,

and I phoned him twice on Thursday and once on Friday.
He must therefore be fully aware that it's his turn, not
    mine.

If I make it too easy for him he'll assume I'm too easy,
while if I make no effort, that leaves him with more of
    a challenge.

I should demonstrate that I have a sense of proportion.
His work must come first for a while and I shouldn't
    mind waiting

For all I know he could have gone off me already
and if I don't phone I can always say, later, that I went
    off him first.

Sophie Hannah

The Most Precious Thing
(A Jewish Folktale)

A merchant lived in Sidon long ago
Who had been married for ten years or so,
Quite happily except for one sad thing –
Their silent home was never known to ring
With children's voices. We today might say
That this was not a tragedy, but they
Felt differently in that far time and place:
To have no heir was viewed as dark disgrace.

And so the husband went with heavy heart
To see the Rabbi and arrange to part
From his dear wife. The Rabbi sadly said,
'So be it. But remember, when you wed,
You held a splendid feast? Well, I commend
That you should also celebrate the end
Of your good marriage with another feast.
You owe that to your faithful wife at least.'

Before the feast began the merchant took
His wife aside and said to her, 'Now look,
I feel so guilty treating you this way.
You know I love you more than words can say,
Yet I must have a child. We've not been blessed,
So we must part. But you must choose the best,
Most precious thing in all the house before
You leave, and you may keep it evermore.'

She smiled her thanks. And when the feast began
She saw he drank more wine than anyone,
And very soon both he and darkness fell;
He drowned in sleep's unfathomable well.
When he awoke he did not recognize
The room in which he lay. To his surprise
His wife came in and kissed his puzzled brow
And said she hoped that he felt better now.

'Where am I?' he exclaimed. 'This room? This bed?'
'You're in my father's house,' she, smiling, said.
'I told the serving men to bring you here.
You said that I could take the thing most dear
And precious from the house. Well, that was you.
You are the dearest thing to me.' He knew
That moment that he could not part from this
Sweet loving wife, so he returned her kiss.

Then off they went to tell the Rabbi; he
Was glad to hear their news and so all three
Knelt and prayed to God that there would be
A child to make complete the couple's joy;
And in the following spring a healthy boy
Was born to them in answer to that prayer,
And happiness, like birdsong, filled the air
And made a second Eden blossom there.

Vernon Scannell

Love and Friendship

Love is like the wild rose-briar,
Friendship is like the holly-tree –
The holly is dark when the rose-briar blooms
But which will bloom most constantly?

The wild rose-briar is sweet in spring,
Its summer blossoms scent the air;
Yet wait till winter comes again
And who will call the wild-briar fair?

Then scorn the silly rose-wreath now
And deck thee with the holly's sheen,
That when December blights thy brow
He still may leave thy garland green.

Emily Brontë

Love Affairs

are like
Californian poppies,

flame-throwers
that burn
out all the colours
in the garden.

Parachutes of silk
turned
upside-down,

red lights
fuelled by the sun,
each black core
buzzing
like an angry bee;

they break

with the weight
of scarlet

Isobel Thrilling

First Frost

A girl is freezing in a telephone booth,
huddled in her flimsy coat,
her face stained by tears
and smeared with lipstick.

She breathes on her thin little fingers.
Fingers like ice. Glass beads in her ears.

She has to beat her way back alone
down the icy street.

First frost. A beginning of losses,
the first frost of telephone phrases.

It is the start of winter glittering on her cheek,
the first frost of having been hurt.

Andrei Voznesensky,
translated by Stanley Kunitz

History

It's only a week but already you are slipping
down the cold black chute of history. Postcards.
Phonecalls. It's like never having seen the Wall,
except in pieces on the dusty shelves of friends.

Once I queued for hours to see the moon in a box
inside a museum, so wild it should have been kept
in a zoo at least but there it was, unremarkable,
a pile of dirt some god had shaken down.

I wait for your letters now: a fleet of strange cargo
with news of changing borders, a heart's small
journeys. They're like the relics of a saint.
Opening the dry white papers is kissing a bone.

Maura Dooley

My True Love

On Monday, Monday,
     My True Love said to me,
'I've brought you this nice pumpkin;
     I picked it off a tree!'

On Tuesday, Tuesday,
     My True Love said to me,
'Look – I've brought you sand tarts;
     I've got them by the sea.'

On Wednesday, Wednesday,
     My True Love said to me,
'I've caught you this white polar bear;
     It came from Tennessee.'

On Thursday, Thursday,
     My True Love said to me,
'This singing yellow butterfly
     I've all for you, from me.'

On Friday, Friday,
  My True Love said to me,
'Here's a long-tailed guinea pig;
  It's frisky as can be.'

On Saturday, Saturday,
  To my True Love I said,
'You have not told me ONE TRUE THING,
  So you I'll never wed!'

Ivy O. Eastwick

Autobiography

Not in the book. She would have thought
to be in the book. Not in the index,
nothing of consequence but honoured by
a footnote or identifying asterisk.

Not in the book the afternoons
in rented rooms when she brought flowers
for the fun of it, for playing at playing house,
to parody the furious surge of love.

There were rooms for five stories over the street
or a staircase down, a basement where
through glass, cement and brick
the traffic hissed.

Not in the book the week of snow
near Lincoln, or the other snow
that slowed a train rolling over Minnesota
on Christmas morning, smoke streaking snow,
black claw mark on the snow,
above the snow a frozen sun.

Not in the book the lies, denials and public tears
or how they would separately leave such rooms
in the city's innocent evening,
defaulters, with the crowd of good intent.

Not in the book where his life's displayed,
arranged, accounted for.

Still she looks for clues, and finds one.
He has smuggled her into a line of print
as once across a frontier. She can close the book.

Elisabeth Riddell

Half

You make the toast, love,
easily on this last day,
feathering it gently
with butter. Accommodating
to the last I chop fresh
red sticks of purest cinnamon
and sprinkle it like confetti
evenly on the toasted slice,
half for you
and half for me.

We eat it smoothly like oil,
Half for you, half for me
and later the furniture too
and even perhaps the children.
Love ends in half.

Karen Hayes

Eating Alone

eating alone
my alphabet soup
speaks to me

Brenda S. Duster

Coat

Sometimes I have wanted
to throw you off
like a heavy coat.

Sometimes I have said
you would not let me
breathe and move.

But now that I am free
to choose light clothes
or none at all

I feel the cold
and all the time I think
how warm it used to be

Vicki Feaver

I So Liked Spring

I so liked Spring last year
     Because you were here;
       The thrushes too –
Because it was these you so liked to hear –
     I so liked you.

    This year's a different thing,
     I'll not think of you.
But I'll like Spring because it is simply Spring
    As the thrushes do.

Charlotte Mew

Ebb

I know what my heart is like
      Since your love died:
It is like a hollow ledge
Holding a little pool
      Left there by the tide,
      A little tepid pool,
Drying inward from the edge.

Edna St Vincent Millay

The 'Darling' Letters

Some keep them in shoeboxes away from the light,
sore memories blinking out as the lid lifts,
their own recklessness written all over them. *My own . . .*
Private jokes, no longer comprehended, pull their
    punchlines,
fall flat in the gaps between endearments. *What are you
    wearing?*

                    Don't ever change.
They start with *Darling*; end in recriminations,
absence, sense of loss. Even now, the fist's bud flowers
into trembling, the fingers trace each line and see
the future then. *Always . . .* Nobody burns them,
the *Darling* letters, stiff in their cardboard coffins.

Babykins . . . We all had strange names
which make us blush, as though we'd murdered
someone under an alias, long ago. *I'll die
without you. Die.* Once in a while, alone,
we take them out to read again, the heart thudding
like a spade on buried bones.

Carol Ann Duffy

Burning Genius

He fell in love with a lady violinist,
It was absurd the lengths he went to to win her affection.
He gave up his job in the Civil Service.
He followed her from concert hall to concert hall,
bought every available biography of Beethoven,
learnt German fluently
brooded over the exact nature of inhuman suffering,
but all to no avail –

Day and night she sat in her attic room,
she sat playing day and night,
oblivious of him,
and even the sparrows that perched on her skylight
        mistaking her music for food.

To impress her, he began to study music in earnest.
Soon he was dismissing Vivaldi and praising Wagner.
He wrote concertos in his spare time,
wrote operas about doomed astronauts and about
   monsters who,
when kissed,
became even more furious and ugly.

He wrote eight symphonies taking care to leave several
   unfinished,

It was exhausting.
And he found no time to return to that attic room.

In fact, he grew old and utterly famous.

And when asked to what he owed
his burning genius,
he shrugged and said little,

but his mind gaped back until he saw before him
the image of a tiny room,
and perched on the skylight the timid
skeletons of sparrows still listened on.

Brian Patten

I'm in the Dark with You

I tried to surround you
forgive me, I'm male
I'm a timid lounge lizard
who's just lost his tail
Now I'm in the dark with you.

I do tend to rush things
It's masculine drive
I'm Romeo on
a King's Cross 125
And I'm in the dark with you.

I'm completely unmoved
by a gloss centrefold
I'm thoroughly houseproud
a new man for old
But I'm still in the dark with you.

Nocturnal confusion,
the silence of doubt,
and how to avoid
being laddish throughout
When I'm here in the dark with you.

Maybe it's hormones, maybe it's fate,
it's certainly gender that gets us in this state
but now all I wish is to stay awake late
and be still, in the dark with you.

Stewart Henderson

Defining the Problem

I can't forgive you. Even if I could
You wouldn't pardon me for seeing through you.
And yet I cannot cure myself of love
For what I thought you were before I knew you.

Wendy Cope

Unfortunate Coincidence

By the time you swear you're his,
         Shivering and sighing,
And he vows his passion is
         Infinite, undying –
Lady, make a note of this:
         One of you is lying.

Dorothy Parker

Half

Three thirty-fivish women met one day,
each well glossed against the others' sharp eyes for flaws.
Old school friends apparently – they slipped
with ease into the former conspiracy of dormitories,
and discussed over coffee and saccharine, the grounds
for divorce. All agreed love made
excessive demands on them,
wondered how long it must be missing
before it could be

              Presumed Dead.

Liz Lochhead

Intimates

Don't you care for my love? she said bitterly.

I handed her the mirror, and said:
Please address these questions to the proper person!
Please make all requests to headquarters!
In all matters of emotional importance
please approach the supreme authority direct!
So I handed her the mirror.

And she would have broken it over my head,
but she caught sight of her own reflection
and that held her spellbound for two seconds
while I fled.

D. H. Lawrence

All That

And then there's the one you write
that makes even you laugh.
You never want to see her again.
You don't want to see her handwriting
on a letter. You don't want to come home
and see the little yellow light
flashing messages of regret.
You don't want to pick up the phone
and hear how much she's been missing you.
Couldn't you meet for a drink?
Not any more. Maybe in a year or two
All you want to do now
is draw a line under your life
and get on with the past.
Do you make yourself perfectly clear?
You sign with just your name,
a businesslike touch
which makes even you laugh.

Hugo Williams

Uphill I Picked Sweet Herbs

Uphill I picked sweet herbs,
Downhill I met my former husband.
Kneeling I asked my former husband,
'Your new one, what is she like then?'
'My new one is good, I suppose,
But not as fine as my old one.
In looks they are like each other,
But their fingernails are not the same.
My new one comes in through the main gates,
My old one would leave through the back door.
My new one is skilled at weaving finespun,
Finespun is forty foot a day,
Homespun was fifty foot or more.
Comparing fineweave and plainweave,
My new one won't match the old!'

Anonymous

Oh, When I Was in Love With You

Oh, when I was in love with you,
    Then I was clean and brave,
And miles around the wonder grew
    How well I did behave.

And now the fancy passes by,
    And nothing will remain,
And miles around they'll say that I
    Am quite myself again.

A. E. Housman

This Is to Let You Know

This is to let you know
That there was no moon last night
And that the tide was high
And that on the broken horizon glimmered the lights
   of ships
Twenty at least, like a sedate procession passing by.

This is to let you know
That when I'd turned out the lamp
And in the dark I lay
That suddenly piercing loneliness, like a knife,
Twisted my heart, for you were such a long long way
   away.

This is to let you know
That there are no English words
That ever could explain
How, quite without warning, lovingly you were here
Holding me close, smoothing away the idiotic pain.
This is to let you know
That all that I feel for you
Can never wholly go.
I love you and miss you, even two hours away,
With all my heart. This is to let you know.

Noel Coward

For Non-Swimmers

A lyric-minded eskimo
sat quietly at his deskimo
and put on paper white as snow
'o eskima I love you so'.

An answer came into his igloo
which ticked him and made him giggloo
and melted all the snow around
until the loving poet drowned.

They dug for him a little hole
and buried him quite near the pole.
His epitaph was short and grim:
'To all the poets: Learn to swim!'

Walter Adamson

Miles Away

I want you and you are not here. I pause
in this garden, breathing the colour thought is
before language into still air. Even your name
is a pale ghost and, though I exhale it again
and again, it will not stay with me. Tonight
I make you up, imagine you, your movements clearer
than the words I have you say you said before.

Wherever you are now, inside my head you fix me
with a look, standing here whilst cool late light
dissolves into the earth. I have got your mouth wrong,
but still it smiles. I hold you closer, miles away,
inventing love, until the calls of nightjars
interrupt and turn what was to come, was certain,
into memory. The stars are filming us for no one.

Carol Ann Duffy

A Call

'Hold on,' she said, 'I'll just run out and get him.
The weather here's so good, he took the chance
To do a bit of weeding.'

        So I saw him
Down on his hands and knees beside the leek rig,
Touching, inspecting, separating one
Stalk from the other, gently pulling up
Everything not tapered, frail and leafless,
Pleased to feel each little weed-root break,
But rueful also . . .

           Then found myself listening to
The amplified grave ticking of hall clocks
Where the phone lay unattended in a calm
Of mirror glass and sunstruck pendulums . . .

And found myself then thinking: if it were nowadays,
This is how Death would summon Everyman.

Next thing he spoke and I nearly said I loved him.

Seamus Heaney

What Lips My Lips Have Kissed

What lips my lips have kissed, and where, and why,
I have forgotten, and what arms have lain
Under my head till morning; but the rain
Is full of ghosts tonight, that tap and sigh
Upon the glass and listen for reply,
And in my heart there sits a quiet pain
For unremembered lads that not again
Will turn to me at midnight with a cry.
Thus in the winter stands the lonely tree,
Nor knows what birds have vanished one by one,
Yet knows its boughs more silent than before:
I cannot say what loves have come and gone;
I only know that summer sang in me
A little while, that in me sings no more.

Edna St Vincent Millay

The Look

Strephon kissed me in the spring,
Robin in the fall,
But Colin only looked at me
And never kissed at all.

Strephon's kiss was lost in jest,
Robin's lost in play,
But the kiss in Colin's eyes
Haunts me night and day.

Sara Teasdale

When You Are Old

When you are old and grey and full of sleep,
And nodding by the fire, take down this book,
And slowly read, and dream of the soft look
Your eyes had once, and of their shadows deep;

How many loved your moments of glad grace,
And loved your beauty with love false or true,
But one man loved the pilgrim soul in you,
And loved the sorrows of your changing face;

And bending down beside the glowing bars,
Murmur, a little sadly, how Love fled
And paced upon the mountains overhead
And hid his face amid a crowd of stars.

W. B. Yeats

Song

Stop all the clocks, cut off the telephone,
Prevent the dog from barking with a juicy bone,
Silence the pianos and with muffled drum
Bring out the coffin, let the mourners come.

Let aeroplanes circle moaning overhead
Scribbling on the sky the message He Is Dead,
Put crêpe bows round the white necks of the public doves,
Let the traffic policemen wear black cotton gloves.

He was my North, my South, my East and West,
My working week and my Sunday rest,
My noon, my midnight, my talk, my song;
I thought that love would last for ever: I was wrong.

The stars are not wanted now: put out every one;
Pack up the moon and dismantle the sun;
Pour away the ocean and sweep up the wood.
For nothing now can ever come to any good.

W. H. Auden

No one

No heart bleeds as red as mine, beloved,
No heart.
No voice sounds as strong as mine, beloved,
No voice.
No eyes see the sun like mine, beloved,
No eyes.
No soul flies so close to you, beloved.
No soul.
No ghost is so close to you, beloved.

Marjolijn Anstey

I Have Lived and I Have Loved

I have lived and I have loved;
I have waked and I have slept;
I have sung and I have danced;
I have smiled and I have wept;
I have won and wasted treasure;
I have had my fill of pleasure;
And all these things were weariness,
And some of them were dreariness.
And all these things – but two things
Were emptiness and pain:
And Love – it was the best of them:
And Sleep – worth all the rest of them.

Anonymous

What Is Love?

Now what is love, I pray thee tell?
It is that fountain and that well
Where pleasure and repentance dwell.
It is perhaps that sauncing bell
That tolls all into heaven or hell:
And this is love, as I hear tell.

Yet what is love, I pray thee say?
It is a work on holy day.
It is December matched with May,
When lusty bloods in fresh array
Hear ten months after of the play:
And this is love, as I hear say.

Yet what is love, I pray thee sain?
It is a sunshine mixed with rain.
It is a toothache, or like pain:
It is a game where none doth gain;
The lass saith No, and would full fain:
And this is love, as I hear sain.

Yet what is love, I pray thee show?
A thing that creeps, it cannot go;
A prize that passeth to and fro;
A thing for one, a thing for mo;
And he that proves must find it so;
And this is love, sweet friend, I trow.

Sir Walter Raleigh

By Sir
walter
Raleigh

Index of First Lines

LoVe   125

Index of Poets

Acknowledgements

The compiler and publishers wish to thank the following for permission to use copyright material:

Marjolijn Anstey, 'No one', by permission of the author; **W. H. Auden**, 'Song' from *Collected Poems* by W. H. Auden (1976), by permission of Faber and Faber Ltd; **John Betjeman**, 'In a Bath Teashop' from *Collected Poems* by John Betjeman, by permission of John Murray (Publishers) Ltd; **Jean 'Binta' Breeze**, 'He Loves My Hair' from *The Arrival of Brighteye* by Jean Binta Breeze (2000), by permission of Bloodaxe Books; **Charles Bukowski**, 'Wearing the Collar' from *You Get So Alone at Times That It Just Makes Sense* by Charles Bukowski (1986). Copyright © 1986 by Charles Bukowski, by permission of Black Sparrow Press; **Gillian Clarke**, 'My Box' from *Collected Poems* by Gillian Clarke (1997), by permission of Carcanet Press Ltd; **Stephen Clarke**, 'Smiling', included in *The Poetry File*, Shropshire, Telford and Wrekin Council (1999), by permission of the author; **Paul Cookson**, ''Till Playtime Do Us Part and the Lovehearts Are All Eaten', first published in *Let No one Steal Your Dreams* by Paul Cookson, A Twist in the Tale (1994), by permission of the author; **Wendy Cope**, 'Flowers' and 'Defining the Problem' from *Serious Concerns* by Wendy Cope (1992), and 'Message' from *Making Cocoa for Kingsley Amis* by Wendy Cope (1986), by permission of Faber and Faber Ltd; **Frances Cornford**, 'The Corner of the Field' from *Collected Verse* by Frances Cornford, by permission of the Trustees of the Estate of the author; **Noel Coward**, 'This Is to Let You Know' from *Collected Verse* by Noel Coward. Copyright © the

Estate of Noel Coward, by permission of Methuen Publishing Ltd; **Maura Dooley**, 'History' from *Kissing a Bone* by Maura Dooley (1996), by permission of Bloodaxe Books; **Carol Ann Duffy**, 'The Duke of Fire and the Duchess of Ice' from *Meeting Midnight* by Carol Ann Duffy (1999), by permission of Faber and Faber Ltd; and 'Miles Away' from *Selling Manhattan* by Carol Ann Duffy (1987), and 'The Darling Letters' from *The Other Country* by Carol Ann Duffy (1990), by permission of Anvil Press Poetry; **Ivy O. Eastwick**, 'My True Love', by permission of Roger Keen; **Gavin Ewart**, 'The Lover Writes a One-Word Poem' from *The Collected Ewart 1933-1980* by Gavin Ewart, by permission of Margo Ewart; **Linda France**, 'If Love Was Jazz' from *Red* by Linda France (1992), by permission of Bloodaxe Books; **Sophie Hannah**, 'The Pros and the Cons' from *Hotels Like Houses* by Sophie Hannah (1996), by permission of Carcanet Press Ltd; **Seamus Heaney**, 'A Call' from *Opened Ground* by Seamus Heaney (1998) by permission of Faber and Faber Ltd; **Stewart Henderson**, 'I'm in the Dark with You' from *Homeland* by Stewart Henderson, Hodder and Stoughton (1993), by permission of the author; **Adrian Henri**, 'I'm in Love with the Weather Lady', first published in *Bloomsbury Book of Love Poems*, Bloomsbury, and 'Party' from *Not Fade Away* by Adrian Henri, Bloodaxe Books (1994). Copyright © 1994 Adrian Henri, by permission of Rogers, Coleridge & White Ltd on behalf of the author; **A. E. Housman**, 'Oh, When I Was in Love With You' from *A Shropshire Lad* by A. E. Housman, by permission of The Society of Authors as the Literary Representative of the Estate of the author; **Jean Kenward**, 'Stepmother', by permission of the author; **Tom Leonard**, 'Words, for E' from *Scottish Love Poems*, ed. Antonia Fraser, by permission of Canongate Books Ltd; **C. Day Lewis**, 'Walking Away' from *The Complete Poems* by C. Day Lewis, Sinclair-Stevenson (1992), by permission of Peters, Fraser and Dunlop Group Ltd on behalf of the Estate of the author; **Liz Lochhead**, 'Half', by permission of The Rod Hall Agency Ltd on behalf of the author; **Hugh McCrae**, 'Song of the Rain' from *Selected Verse* by Hugh McCrea, ETT Imprint, Sydney (1992), by permission of ETT Imprint; **Roger McGough**, 'The Railings' from *Defying Gravity* by Roger McGough, Viking Penguin (1992), and 'The Icingbus' and 'My cat and i' from *The Mersey Sound* by Roger McGough, Jonathan Cape, by permission of Peters Fraser & Dunlop Group Ltd on behalf of the author; **Charlotte Mew**, 'I So Liked Spring' from *Collected Poems and Selected Prose* by Charlotte Mew, by permission of Carcanet Press Ltd; **Edna St Vincent Millay**, 'Ebb' and 'What Lips My Lips Have Kissed' from *What Lips My Lips Have Kissed* by Edna St Vincent Millay, by permission of A. M. Heath and Co on behalf of the author; **Spike Milligan**, 'Love Song' from *Small Dreams of a Scorpion* by Spike Milligan, by permission of Spike Milligan Productions; **John Mole**, 'Taking the Plunge' from *Boo to a Goose* by John Mole, Peterloo Poets (1987), and 'First Love' from *Hot Air* by John Mole, Hodder & Stoughton (1996), by permission of the author; **Edwin Muir**, 'The Confirmation' from *Collected Poems* by Edwin Muir, by permission of Faber and Faber Ltd; **Judith Nicholls**, 'Sea Song' from *Magic Mirror* by Judith Nicholls, Faber and Faber Ltd (1985). Copyright © 1985 Judith Nicholls, by permission of the author; **Grace Nichols**, 'Like a Flame' from *The Fat Black Lady's Poems* (1984), by permission of Curtis Brown Ltd, London, on behalf of the author; Dorothy Parker, 'Unfortunate Coincidence' from *Collected Dorothy Parker* by Dorothy Parker (1973), by permission of Gerald Duckworth & Co Ltd; **Brian Patten**, 'Burning Genius' from *Love Poems* by Brian Patten, George Allen & Unwin. Copyright © Brian Patten 1981, by permission of Rogers Coleridge and White on behalf of the author; **Joan Poulson**,

'First Kiss', by permission of the author; **Elisabeth Riddell**, 'Autobiography' from *Selected Poems* by Elisabeth Riddell, ETT Imprint, Sydney, by permission of ETT Imprint; **Philip Ridley**, 'The Silver Hat', by permission of A. P. Watt Ltd on behalf of the author; **Vernon Scannell**, 'The Power of Love', 'The Most Precious Thing' and 'Growing Pain' from *Love, Shouts and Whispers* by Vernon Scannell, Hutchinson (1990), by permission of the author; **Fred Sedgwick**, 'Two Small Boys and an Elephant' from *Blind Date* by Fred Sedgwick, Tricky Sam (1999), by permission of the author; **Stevie Smith**, 'Human Affection' from *The Collected Poems of Stevie Smith* by Stevie Smith, by permission of the Executors of James MacGibbon; **Stephen Spender**, 'To My Daughter' from *Collected Poems* by Stephen Spender, by permission of Faber and Faber Ltd; **Isobel Thrilling**, 'Love Affairs', by permission of the author; **Judith Viorst**, 'Lizzie Pitofsky Poem' from *If I Were in Charge of the World and Other Worries*, Atheneum (1981), Copyright © Judith Viorst 1981, by permission of A. M. Heath & Co Ltd on behalf of the author; **Dave Ward**, 'I'd Never Fall in Love with a Girl', by permission of the author; **Hugo Williams**, 'All That' from Billy's Rain by Hugo Williams (1999), by permission of Faber and Faber Ltd; **W. B. Yeats**, 'When You Are Old', by permission of A. P. Watt Ltd on behalf of Michael B. Yeats.

Every effort has been made to trace the copyright holders but if any have been inadvertently overlooked, the publishers will be pleased to make the necessary arrangement at the first opportunity.